ST. MARY'S COLL
ST. MARY'

S0-AEG-744

Alice S. Clendinen -
from. Rosalie -

Christmas 1932 - Radnor.

BOOKS BY WILLIAM J. JOHNSTONE

———

HOW WASHINGTON PRAYED
GEORGE WASHINGTON THE CHRISTIAN
ABRAHAM LINCOLN THE CHRISTIAN
HOW LINCOLN PRAYED

WASHINGTON'S PRAYER AT VALLEY FORGE

LIBRARY
St. Mary's Seminary - Junior College

How Washington Prayed

WILLIAM J. JOHNSTONE

THE ABINGDON PRESS

NEW YORK   CINCINNATI   CHICAGO

Copyright, 1932, by
WILLIAM J. JOHNSTONE

All rights reserved—no part of this book may be reproduced in any
form without permission in writing from the publisher.

8800

Printed in the United States of America

DEDICATED

TO

MY GRANDDAUGHTERS

YVONNE LUCILE HAUSER

RUTH ALLYNE HILLMAN

"Behold, he prayeth."—Acts 9. 11

PREFACE

"A GREAT general like Napoleon may be produced in a military school. A great diplomatist like Metternich may be developed in a court. A great philosopher like Hegel may be evolved in a university. But a great man like Washington can only come from a Christian home."

The American people owe a debt of gratitude to the mother of George Washington. "From her loving arms he was received into the church in baptism. And she was careful to see that he 'was virtuously brought up to lead a godly and a Christian life.'" When he left the home of his youth, her last words to him were, "My son, neglect not the duty of secret prayer."

Washington faithfully followed his mother's injunction. We have testimony to his daily devotions for forty-five years, from his twenty-third year to his death. "It was his habit while engaged in the French and Indian War; it was also during the Revolutionary War; and it was the same during his

Presidential terms, and no doubt it was so
to the end of his life." Lincoln once said,
"I have kept up the habit of daily prayer
since coming to the White House." Washington and Lincoln spent a part of every day
in prayer and reading the Bible.

Through all his course of trials and temptations, in adversity and prosperity, in the
home, in the field, in public office, Washington was an humble worshiper of God, and
daily sought his wisdom and guidance.

"It is no wonder that the Americans con-
quered, when their leader was a man of so
much faith and prayer. Here was the great
secret of their success. Washington believed
in God, and in his providence and government among nations; and believing that his
country's cause was a just and right one, he
carried it before the Lord, and asked his aid
in its vindication and support. The good
man's prayer was heard; victory perched
upon the American banner, and the United
colonies became free and independent
states."

People have been interested in the brilliant
military and political life of George Washington without asking what was the spiritual

secret of it.   The highest side of his life has not received sufficient attention.

I now present to you, "Washington, the Man of Prayer," a supreme example in duty and inspiration.

The incidents in his prayer-life are arranged chronologically, as far as possible.

W. J. Johnstone

HOW WASHINGTON PRAYED

The Family Tree

"Every good tree bringeth forth good fruit" (Matthew 7. 17). Thus spake the Great Teacher nineteen centuries ago.

It was by the Christian training of the child that the Washingtons prepared the way for the greatest single achievement in their family and also for generations of happiness and usefulness. The children were brought up in the church for generation after generation. A sincere devotion to the church which began long before George Washington was born, and long before the Reformation, maintained itself in an unbroken line to the present day.

There was a strong family inclination to service in the ministry. George's great-great-grandfather, the Rev. L a w r e n c e Washington, was a clergyman in the Church of England, Vicar of Purleigh in Essex, and afterward Vicar of Tring. He had a good many relatives who were ordained ministers: the Rev. Lawrence Washington, who was

University preacher in 1570; the Rev. Lawrence Washington, Vicar of Colmer, who died in 1610; the Rev. Lawrence Washington, Vicar of Stotesbury, who died in 1619. That the family in England continued its ministerial record is shown by the fact that Admiral John Washington was the father of the Rev. George Washington. Among his descendants were the Rev. Adam Washington, the Rev. Marmaduke Washington, and the Rev. Henry Washington.

One of the descendants of the first Rev. Lawrence Washington estimates that ninety-five per cent of his twelve hundred American descendants have proven themselves faithful children of God and good brothers of men. They are still found on the vestries of Virginia churches. One of them is the Bishop of Tokyo.

CHILDHOOD HOME

The Washington home was a religious home. The father and mother of George Washington were members of the Church of England, almost the only denomination of Christians at that time in Virginia. Everybody in that region went to church whenever

there was service. In childhood George
formed the habit of regular attendance at
church, and of participating in the worship.
He received from his parents daily instruc-
tion in the Bible and the *Prayer Book*.

A Young Man's Prayers

On April 21, 22, 23, 1891, there was sold
at auction in Philadelphia a remarkable col-
lection of Washington relics owned by Lawrence Washington, Bushrod C. Washington, Thomas B. Washington, and J. R. C.
Lewis. Among them was found a little
manuscript book entitled *The Daily Sacrifice,* which Washington left in his library at
Mount Vernon.

"This gem is all in the handwriting of
George Washington, when about twenty
years old, and is, without exception, the most
hallowed of all his writings. It is neatly
written on twenty-four pages of a little book
about the size of the ordinary pocket memorandum."[1]

"The occasional interlineations and emen-
dations indicate that it was prepared for his
own use."

Whether Washington composed t h e

prayers himself or copied them from some source as yet unknown has not been determined; but they are a revelation of that striking character which has been the wonder of the world. The late Professor S. F. Upham, professor of practical theology in Drew Theological Seminary, wrote: "The 'Daily Prayers' of George Washington abound in earnest thought, expressed in simple, beautiful, fervent and evangelical language. They reveal to us the real life of the great patriot, and attest his piety. None can read those petitions, which bore his desires to God, and often brought answers of peace, without having a grander conception of Washington's character."

"The prayers are characterized by a deep consciousness of sin and by a recognition of dependence upon the merits and mercies of our Lord. They contain fervent supplications for family, friends, and rulers in church and state." The prayers, reprinted by special permission of Rev. Dr. W. Herbert Burk, are as follows:

(1) *Sunday Morning*

Almighty God, and most merciful father, who

didst command the children of Israel to offer a
daily sacrifice to thee, that thereby they might
glorify and praise thee for thy protection both
night and day; receive, O Lord, my morning sacrifice which I now offer up to thee; I yield thee
humble and hearty thanks that thou hast pre-
served me from the dangers of the night past,
and brought me to the light of this day, and the
comforts thereof, a day which is consecrated to
thine own service and for thine own service and
for thine own honor. Let my heart, therefore,
Gracious God, be so affected with the glory and
majesty of it, that I may not do mine own works,
but wait on thee, and discharge those weighty
duties thou requirest of me; and since thou art a
God of pure eyes, and wilt be sanctified in all who
draw near unto thee, who doest not regard the
sacrifice of fools, nor hear sinners who tread in
thy courts, pardon, I beseech thee, my sins, re-
move them from my presence, as far as the east is
from the west, and accept of me for the merits
of thy son Jesus Christ, that when I come into
thy temple, and compass thine altar, my prayers
may come before thee as incense; and as thou
wouldst hear me calling upon thee in my prayers,
so give me grace to hear thee calling on me in thy
word, that it may be wisdom, righteousness, reconciliation, and peace to the saving of my soul in
the day of the Lord Jesus. Grant that I may
hear it with reverence, receive it with meekness,
mingle it with faith, and that it may accomplish

in me, Gracious God, the good work for which
thou hast sent it. Bless my family, kindred,
friends and country, be our God & guide this day
and for ever for his sake, who lay down in the
Grave and rose again for us, Jesus Christ our
Lord, Amen.

(2) *Sunday Evening*

O most Glorious God, in Jesus Christ my merciful and loving father, I acknowledge and confess
my guilt, in the weak and imperfect performance
of the duties of this day. I have called on thee
for pardon and forgiveness of sins, but so coldly
and carelessly, that my prayers are become my
sin and stand in need of pardon. I have heard
thy holy word, but with such deadness of spirit
that I have been an unprofitable and forgetful
hearer, so that, O Lord, tho' I have done thy
work, yet it hath been so negligently that I may
rather expect a curse than a blessing from thee.
But, O God, who art rich in mercy and plenteous
in redemption, mark not, I beseech thee, what I
have done amiss; remember that I am but dust,
and remit my transgressions, negligences, & ig-
norances, and cover them all with the absolute
obedience of thy dear Son, that those sacrifices
which I have offered may be accepted by thee, in
and for the sacrifice of Jesus Christ offered upon
the cross for me; for his sake, ease me of the
burden of my sins, and give me grace that by the
call of the Gospel I may rise from the slumber

of sin into the newness of life. Let me live according to those holy rules which thou hast this day prescribed in thy holy word; make me to know what is acceptable in thy sight, and therein to delight, open the eyes of my understanding, and help me thoroughly to examine myself concerning my knowledge, faith and repentance; increase my faith, and direct me to the true object Jesus Christ the way, the truth and the life; bless, O Lord, all the people of this land, from the highest to the lowest, particularly those whom thou hast appointed to rule over us in church & state. continue thy goodness to me this night. These weak petitions I humbly implore thee to hear accept and ans. for the sake of thy Dear Son Jesus Christ our Lord, Amen.

(3) *Monday Morning*

O eternal and everlasting God, I presume to present myself this morning before thy Divine majesty, beseeching thee to accept of my humble and hearty thanks, that it hath pleased thy great goodness to keep and preserve me the night past from all the dangers poor mortals are subject to, and has given me sweet and pleasant sleep, whereby I find my body refreshed and comforted for performing the duties of this day, in which I beseech thee to defend me from all perils of body and soul. Direct my thoughts, words and work, wash away my sins in the immaculate blood of the lamb, and purge my heart by thy holy spirit, from the dross of my natural corruption, that I may with more freedom of mind and liberty of will serve thee, the ever lasting God, in righteousness and holiness this day, and all the days of my life. Increase my faith in the sweet promises of the gospel; give me repentance from dead works; pardon my wanderings, & direct my thoughts unto thyself, the God of my salvation; teach me how to live in thy fear, labor in thy service, and ever to run in the ways of thy commandments; make me always watchful over my heart, that neither the terrors of conscience, the loathing of holy duties, the love of sin, nor unwillingness to depart this life, may cast me into a spiritual slumber, but daily frame me more & more into the likeness of thy son Jesus Christ, that living in thy fear, and dying in thy favor, I may in thy appointed time attain the resurrection of the just unto eternal life bless my family, friends & kindred unite us all in praising & glorifying thee in all our works begun, continued, and ended, when we shall come to make our last account before thee blessed saviour, who hath taught us to pray, our Father, &c.

(4) *Monday Evening*

Most Gracious Lord God, from whom proceedeth every good and perfect gift, I offer to thy divine majesty my unfeigned praise & thanksgiving for all thy mercies towards me. Thou mad'st me at first and hast ever since sustained

the work of thy own hand; thou gav'st thy Son
to die for me; and hast given me assurance of
salvation, upon my repentance and sincerely endeavoring to conform my life to his holy precepts
and example. Thou art pleased to lengthen out
to me the time of repentance and to move me to
it by thy spirit and by thy word, by thy mercies,
and by thy judgments; out of a deepness of thy
mercies, and my own unworthiness, I do appear
before thee at this time; I have sinned and done
very wickedly; be merciful to me, O God, and pardon me for Jesus Christ sake; instruct me in the
particulars of my duty, and suffer me not to be
temped above what thou givest me strength to
bear. Take care, I pray thee of my affairs and
more and more direct me in thy truth, defend
me from my enemies, especially spiritual ones.
Suffer me not to be drawn from thee, by the blan-
dishments of the world, carnal desires, the cun-
ning of the devil, or deceitfulness of sin. work in
me thy good will and pleasure, and discharge my
mind from all things that are displeasing to thee,
of all ill will and discontent, wrath and bitter-
ness, pride & vain conceit of myself, and render
me charitable, pure, holy, patient and heavenly
minded. be with me at the hour of death; dispose
me for it, and deliver me from the slavish fear
of it, and make me willing and fit to die whenever
thou shalt call me hence. Bless our rulers in
church and state. bless O Lord the whole race of
mankind, and let the world be filled with the knowl-

edge of Thee and thy son Jesus Christ. Pity
the sick, the poor, the weak, the needy, the widows
and fatherless, and all that morn or are broken
in heart, and be merciful to them according to
their several necessities. bless my friends and
grant me grace to forgive my enemies as heartily
as I desire forgiveness of Thee my heavenly
Father. I beseech thee to defend me this night
from all evil, and do more for me than I can think
or ask, for Jesus Christ sake, in whose most holy
name & words, I continue to pray, Our Father, &c.

(5) *Tuesday Morning*

O Lord our God, most mighty and merciful
father, I thine unworthy creature and servant, do
once more approach thy presence. Though not
worthy to appear before thee, because of my
natural corruptions, and the many sins and transgressions which I have committed against thy
divine majesty; yet I beseech thee, for the sake
of him in whom thou art well pleased, the Lord
Jesus Christ, to admit me to render thee deserved
thanks and praises for thy manifold mercies extended toward me, for the quiet rest & repose of
the past night, for food, raiment, health, peace,
liberty, and the hopes of a better life through the
merits of thy dear son's bitter passion. and O
kind father continue thy mercy and favor to me
this day, and ever hereafter; prosper all my law-
ful undertakings; let me have all my directions
from thy holy spirit, and success from thy bounti-

ful hand. Let the bright beams of thy light so
shine into my heart, and enlighten my mind in
understanding thy blessed word, that I may be
enabled to perform thy will in all things, and
effectually resist all temptations of the world, the
flesh and the devil. preserve and defend our
rulers in church & state. bless the people of this
land, be a father to the fatherless, a comforter
to the comfortless, a deliverer to the captives, and
a physician to the sick. let thy blessings be upon
friends, kindred and families. Be our guide this
day and forever through J. C. in whose blessed
form of prayer I conclude my weak petitions—
—Our Father, &c.

(6) *Tuesday Evening*

Most Gracious God and heavenly father, we
cannot cease, but must cry unto thee for mercy,
because my sins cry against me for justice. How
shall I address myself unto thee, I must with the
publican stand and admire at thy great goodness,
tender mercy, and long suffering towards me, in
that thou hast kept me the past day from being
consumed and brought to nought. O Lord, what
is man, or the son of man, that thou regardest
him; the more days pass over my head, the more
sins and iniquities I heap up against thee. If I
should cast up the account of my good deeds
done this day, how few and small would they be;
but if I should reckon my miscarriages, surely
they would be many and great. O, blessed Father,

let thy son's blood wash me from all impurities, and cleanse me from the stains of sin that are upon me. Give me grace to lay hold upon his merits; that they may be my reconciliation and atonement unto thee,—That I may know my sins are forgiven by his death & passion. embrace me in the arms of thy mercy; vouchsafe to receive me unto the bosom of thy love, shadow me with thy wings, that I may safely rest under thy protection this night; and so into thy hands I commend myself, both soul and body, in the name of thy son, J. C., beseeching Thee, when this life shall end, I may take my everlasting rest with thee in thy heavenly kingdom. bless all in authority over us, be merciful to all those afflicted with thy cross or calamity, bless all my friends, forgive my enemies and accept my thanksgiving this evening for all the mercies and favors afforded me; hear and graciously answer these my requests, and whatever else thou see'st needful grant us, for the sake of Jesus Christ in whose blessed name and words I continue to pray, Our Father, &c.

(7) *A Prayer for Wednesday Morning*

Almighty and eternal Lord God, the great creator of heaven & earth, and the God and Father of our Lord Jesus Christ; look down from heaven, in pity and compassion upon me thy servant, who humbly prostrate myself before thee, sensible of thy mercy and my own misery; there

is an infinite distance between thy glorious majesty and me, thy poor creature, the work of
thy hand, between thy infinite power, and my
weakness, thy wisdom, and my folly, thy eternal
Being, and my mortal frame, but, O Lord, I have
set myself at a greater distance from thee by my
sin and wickedness, and humbly acknowledge the
corruption of my nature and the many rebellions
of my life. I have sinned against heaven and before thee, in thought, word & deed; I have con-
temned thy majesty and holy laws. I have like-
wise sinned by omitting what I ought to have done,
and committing what I ought not. I have rebelled
against light, despised thy mercies and judgments, and broken my vows and promises; I have
neglected the means of Grace, and opportunities
of becoming better; my iniquities are multiplied,
and my sins are very great. I confess them, O
Lord, with shame and sorrow, detestation and
loathing, and desire to be vile in my own eyes,
as I have rendered myself vile in thine. I humbly
beseech thee to be merciful to me in the free pardon of my sins, for the sake of thy dear Son,
my only saviour, J. C., who came not to call
the righteous, but sinners to repentance; be
pleased to renew my nature and write thy laws
upon my heart, and help me to live, righteously,
soberly and godly in this evil world; make me
humble, meek, patient and contented, and work
in me the grace of thy holy spirit. prepare me
for death and judgment, and let the thoughts

thereof awaken me to a greater care and study to approve myself unto thee in well doing. bless our rulers in church & state. Help all in affliction or adversity—give them patience and a sanctified use of their affliction, and in thy good time deliverance from them; forgive my enemies, take me unto thy protection this day, keep me in perfect peace, which I ask in the name & for the sake of Jesus. Amen.

(8) *Wednesday Evening*

Holy and eternal Lord God who art the King of heaven, and the watchman of Israel, that never slumberest or sleepest, what shall we render unto thee for all thy benefits; because thou hast inclined thine ears unto me, therefore will I call on thee as long as I live, from the rising of the sun to the going down of the same let thy name be praised. among the infinite riches of thy mercy towards me, I desire to render thanks & praise for thy merciful preservation of me this day, as well as all the days of my life; and for the many other blessings & mercies spiritual & temporal which thou hast bestowed on me, contrary to my deserving. All these thy mercies call on me to be thankful and my infirmities & wants call for a continuance of thy tender mercies; cleanse my soul, O Lord, I beseech thee, from whatever is offensive to thee, and hurtful to me, and give me what is convenient for me, watch over me this night, and give me comfortable sweet sleep to fit

me for the service of the day following. Let my
soul watch for the coming of the Lord Jesus; let
my bed put me in mind of my grave, and my
rising from there of my last resurrection; O
heavenly Father, so frame this heart of mine, that
I may ever delight to live according to thy will
and command, in holiness and righteousness before thee all the days of my life. Let me remember, O Lord, the time will come when the trumpet
shall sound, and the dead shall arise and stand
before the judgment seat, and give an account
of whatever they have done in the body, and let
me so prepare my soul, that I may do it with
joy and not with grief. bless the rulers and
people of this land and forget not those who are
under any affliction or oppression. Let thy favor
be extended to all my relations friends and all
others who I ought to remember in my prayer and
hear me I beseech thee for the sake of my dear
redeemer in whose most holy words, I farther
pray, Our Father, &c.

(9) *Thursday Morning*

Most gracious Lord God, whose dwelling is in
the highest heavens, and yet beholdest the lowly
and humble upon earth, I blush and am ashamed
to lift up my eyes to thy dwelling place, because
I have sinned against thee; look down, I beseech
thee upon me thy unworthy servant who prostrate myself at the footstool of mercy, confessing
my own guiltiness, and begging pardon for my

sins; what couldst thou have done Lord more for me, or what could I have done more against thee? Thou didst send me thy Son to take our nature upon

Note: The manuscript ended at this place, the close of a page. Whether the other pages were lost or the prayers were never completed, has not been determined.

MOTHER'S ADVICE

When Washington was twenty-one years of age—1753—he was commissioned by the governor of Virginia to carry dispatches to the French commander in western Pennsylvania, near the present site of Pittsburgh. He called to see his mother and explained the nature of his mission. As he was leaving, his mother repeated what she had said to him before—"My son, neglect not the duty of secret prayer." Never did a mother give better advice to her son, and never did a son more conscientiously follow it. It seems to have been his uniform practice throughout his whole life.[2]

LAY READER

Washington was a lay reader of the Episcopal Church in the French and Indian

War. While occupying Fort Necessity, during the encampment at Great Meadows in 1754, it was his practice to have the troops assembled for public worship, and it was his custom to have prayers in the camp.[3]

Colonel B. Temple, who was one of his aides in the French and Indian War, said that he had "frequently known Washington, on the Sabbath, to read the Scriptures and pray with his regiment, in the absence of the chaplain."[4]

Prays With Indians

At this time, Mr. Fairfax, father-in-law of Lawrence Washington, b r o t h e r o f George, wrote Washington, saying:

I will not doubt your having public prayers in the camp, especially where the Indian families are your guests, that they, seeing your plain manner of worship, may have their curiosity excited to be informed why we do not use the ceremonies of the French, which being well explained to their understandings, will more and more dispose them to receive our baptism, and unite in strict bonds of cordial friendship.[5]

It certainly was not one of the least striking pictures presented in this wild campaign—the youthful commander, presiding with calm seriousness over a motley assemblage of half-equipped soldiery, leathern-clad hunters and woodsmen, and painted savages with their wives and children, and uniting them all in solemn devotion by his own example and demeanor.[6]

PRAYS FOR DYING STEPDAUGHTER

Mrs. Washington's only remaining daughter [Martha] died on June 19, 1773, at the age of sixteen. She was naturally of a frail constitution, and had for many months been gradually fading away. The heat of summer seemed rapidly to develop the seeds of consumption which were lurking in her system, and when her affectionate stepfather, the only father she had ever known, returned home, after a short absence at Williamsburg on public duty, he was shocked to discover the change. The tender and doting mother, upon whose watchful care the prolonged illness of the feeble child had made large drafts, was nearly over-whelmed with grief, and Washington, falling on his knees at the bedside, with a passionate burst of tears, prayed aloud most fervently, most affectingly, that the loved one might be spared.   Judge Washington's

mother and other witnesses bear testimony
to this. "Upon the wings of that holy prayer
her spirit ascended, and when he arose and
looked upon her pale and placid face, death
had set its seal there." He had the assured
hope of her eternal happiness.

"The sweet, innocent girl," Washington
wrote, "entered into a more happy and
peaceful abode than she had met with in the
afflicted path she had hitherto trod."[7]

Kneels During Prayer

September 1, 1774, Washington left home
for Philadelphia as a member from Virginia
of the First Continental Congress about to
meet in that city. It met on the fifth. The
first two days were spent in organizing and
arranging preliminaries, when it was pro-
posed that the sessions should be opened
with prayer. The Rev. Jacob Duché, an
Episcopal clergyman, was invited to officiate.
The first morning, September 7, 1774, he
read the thirty-fifth psalm, which begins as
follows:

"Plead my cause, O Lord, with them that
strive with me: fight against them that fight
against me.

"Take hold of shield and buckler, and stand up for mine help.

"Draw out also the spear, and stop the way against them that persecute me: say unto my soul, I am thy salvation."

After the psalm, Mr. Duché offered the following prayer:

O Lord, our Heavenly Father, high and mighty King of kings and Lord of lords, who dost from thy throne behold all the dwellers on earth, and reignest with power supreme and uncontrolled over all kingdoms, empires, and governments; look down in mercy we beseech thee, on these American States, who have fled to thee from the rod of the oppressor, and thrown themselves on thy gracious protection, desiring to be henceforth dependent only on thee; to thee they have appealed for the righteousness of their cause; to thee do they now look up for that countenance and support which thou alone canst give; take them, therefore, Heavenly Father, under thy nurturing care; give them wisdom in council, and valor in the field; defeat the malicious designs of our cruel adversaries, convince them of the unrighteousness of their cause; and if they still persist in their sanguinary purposes, O let the voice of thine own unerring justice sounding in their hearts constrain them to drop the weapons of war from their unnerved hands in the day of battle. Be thou present, O God of wisdom, and direct the councils of this honorable assembly; enable them to settle things on the best and surest foundation, that the scene of blood may be speedily closed, that order, harmony, and peace, may be effectually restored; and truth and justice, religion and piety, prevail and flourish amongst thy people. Preserve the health of their bodies and the vigor of their minds; shower down on them and the millions they here represent such temporal blessings as thou seest expedient for them in this world and crown them with everlasting glory in the world to come. All this we ask in the name and through the merits of Jesus Christ, thy Son, our Saviour. Amen.[8]

John Adams, in a letter to his wife on the day following, thus describes the scene:

You must remember this was the morning after we heard the horrible rumor of the cannonade of Boston. I never saw a greater effect upon an audience. It seemed as if Heaven had ordained that psalm to be read on that morning. After this Mr. Duché unexpectedly to everybody struck out into an extemporary prayer, which filled the bosom of every man present. Episcopalian as he is, Doctor Cooper himself never prayed with such fervor, such ardor, such earnestness and pathos, and in language so eloquent and sublime, for America, for the Congress, for the province of Massachusetts Bay, and especially the town of Boston. It had an excellent effect upon every-body here.[9]

"Washington was kneeling, and Henry, and Randolph, and Rutledge, and Lee, and Jay, and by their sides there stood, bowed in reverence, the Puritan patriots of New England."

A gentleman asked Mr. Secretary Thompson how he should be able to know Washington. Mr. Thompson replied: "You can easily distinguish him when Congress goes to prayer. Mr. Washington is the gentleman who always kneels down during prayer."[10]

Prays Before Battle

It is said that just before the engagement on the battlefield of Chatterton Hill, October 28, 1776, Washington knelt in the home where he was entertained, and wrestled in prayer with the God of battles:

His loyal heart, stung with the epithet "rebel," hurled at patriots, was, at the family altar, poured out into the language of the very "Bible hero without a flaw" he is said to resemble. His words were those of the twenty-second verse of chapter 22 of the book of Joshua: "The Lord

God of gods, he knoweth, and Israel he shall know; if it be in rebellion, or if in transgression against the Lord."[11]

Prayer at Valley Forge

In the winter of 1777-78, the American army was encamped at Valley Forge, Pennsylvania. Washington had his quarters in the home of Isaac Potts, the miller, a Quaker minister and a Tory. Mrs. Washington was there, and some officers. There was not much room for privacy. Washington was frequently observed to visit a secluded grove near by. One day Mr. Potts "strolled up the creek, when he heard a solemn voice. He walked quietly in the direction of it, and saw Washington's horse tied to a sapling. In a thicket near by was the beloved chief upon his knees in prayer, his cheeks suffused with tears."[12]

Mr. Potts then returned, and said to his family, *"Our* cause is *lost"* (he was with the Tories). He gave his reasons for this change of opinion:

I have this day seen what I never expected. Thee knows that I always thought that the sword and the gospel were utterly inconsistent; and that

no man could be a soldier and a Christian at the
same time. But George Washington has this day
convinced me of my mistake.

If George Washington be not a man of God,
I am greatly deceived—and still more shall I
be deceived, if God does not, through him, work
out a great salvation for America.[13]

If there is any one on this earth whom the Lord
will listen to, it is George Washington; and I
feel a presentiment that under such a commander
there can be no doubt of our eventually establish-
ing our independence, and that God in his providence has willed it so.[14]

This event induced Friend Potts to become a Whig. He told his wife Betty that
the cause of America was a good cause, and
would prevail, and that they must now support it.[15]

Few scenes have had so much moral grandeur
in them as this. Repeated disaster and defeat
had disappointed the army and the nation. Suffering, to an extreme degree, was in the camp,
and thousands of brave men were without the
necessities of life. The independence of the nation
was in jeopardy. Attempts were made to stab
the reputation of the commander, and to degrade
him from office. Provision for the army was to
be made, murmurs and discontents suppressed,
calumny to be met, plans formed for a future

campaign, the nation to be inspirited and aroused; an active enemy was in the neighborhood, flushed with recent victory, and preparing to achieve new triumphs; and in these circumstances the Father of his Country went alone and sought strength and guidance from the God of armies and light. The ear of Heaven was propitious to his prayer; and who can tell how much of the subsequent brilliant success of the American armies was in answer to the prayers of the American general at Valley Forge?[16]

A Stranger in the House

The Rev. E. C. M'Guire, often quoted in this volume, relates an additional instance of Washington engaged in prayer during the war, taken, he says, from a respectable literary journal published in New York. It is here inserted as having in its prominent points all the appearance of truth:

One pleasant evening in the month of June, in the year 1779 (?), a man was observed entering the borders of a wood, near Hudson River, his appearance that of a person above the common rank. The inhabitants of a country village would have dignified him with the title of squire, and from his manner, have pronounced him proud; but those more accustomed to society would inform you there was something like a military air about him. His horse panted as if it had been hard pushed for some miles, yet from the owner's frequent stops to caress the patient animal, he could not be charged with want of humanity, but seemed to be actuated by some urgent necessity. The rider's forsaking a good road for the bypath leading through the woods indicated a desire to avoid the gaze of other travelers. He had not left the house where he inquired the direction of the above mentioned path more than two hours before the quietude of the place was broken by the noise of distant thunder. He was soon after obliged to dismount, traveling becoming dangerous, as darkness concealed surrounding objects, except when the lightning's terrific flash afforded a momentary view of his situation. A peal of louder and longer duration than any of the preceding, which now burst over his head, seeming as if it would rend the woods asunder, was quickly followed by a heavy fall of rain, which penetrated the clothing of the stranger ere he could obtain shelter of a large oak, which stood at a little distance.

Almost exhausted with the labors of the day, he was about making such disposition of the saddle and his coat as would enable him to pass the night with what comfort circumstances would admit, when he espied a light glimmering through the trees. Animated with the hope of better lodgings, he determined to proceed. The way, which was somewhat steep, became attended with more obstacles the farther he advanced, the soil being composed of clay, which the rain had rendered so soft that his feet slipped at every step. By the utmost perseverance, this difficulty was finally overcome without any accident, and he had the pleasure of finding himself in front of a decent-looking farmhouse. The watchdog began barking, which brought the owner of the mansion to the door.

"Who is there?" said he.

"A friend who has lost his way, and in search of a place of shelter," was the answer.

"Come in, sir," added the first speaker, "and whatever my house will afford, you shall have with welcome."

"I must first provide for the weary companion of my journey," remarked the other.

But the farmer undertook the task, and after conducting the newcomer into a room where his wife was seated, he led the horse to a well-stored barn, and there provided for him most bountifully. On rejoining the traveler he observed, "That is a noble animal of yours, sir."

"Yes," was the reply, "and I am sorry that I was obliged to misuse him so, as to make it necessary to give you much trouble with the care of him; but I have yet to thank you for your kindness to both of us."

"I did no more than my duty, sir," said the entertainer, "and therefore I am entitled to no thanks. But, Susan," added he, turning to the hostess, with a half-reproachful look, "why have you not given the gentleman something to eat?"

Fear had prevented the good woman from exercising her well-known benevolence, for a robbery had been committed by a lawless band of depredators but a few days before, in that neighborhood, and as report stated that the ruffians were all well dressed, her imagination suggested that this man might be one of them. Naturally she would be on her guard.

At her husband's remonstrance, she now readily engaged in repairing her error, by preparing a plentiful repast. During the meal, there was much interesting conversation among the three. As soon as the worthy countryman perceived that his guest had satisfied his appetite he informed him that it was now the hour at which the family usually performed their evening devotions, inviting him at the same time to be present. The invitation was accepted in these words:

"It would afford me the greatest pleasure to commune with my heavenly Preserver, after the events of the day; such exercises prepare us for the repose we seek in sleep."

The host now reached his Bible from the shelf, and after reading a chapter and singing, concluded the whole with a fervent prayer; then lighting a pine-knot, conducted the person he had entertained to his chamber, wished him a good night's rest, and retired to the adjoining apartment.

"John," whispered the woman, "that is a good

gentleman, and not one of the highwaymen as I supposed."

"Yes, Susan," said he, "I like him better for thinking of his God, than for all his kind inquiries after our welfare. I wish our Peter had been home from the army, if it was only to hear this good man talk; I am sure Washington himself could not say more for his country, nor give a better history of the hardships endured by our brave soldiers."

"Who knows now," inquired the wife, "but it may be he himself, after all, my dear, for they do say, he travels just so, all alone, sometimes. Hark! what's that?"

The sound of a voice came from the chamber of their guest, who was now engaged in his private religious worship. After thanking the Creator for his many mercies, and asking a blessing on the inhabitants of the house, he continued: "And now, Almighty Father, if it be thy holy will, that we shall obtain a place and a name among the nations of the earth, grant that we may be enabled to show our gratitude for thy goodness, by our endeavors to fear and obey thee. Bless us with wisdom in our councils, success in battle, and let all our victories be tempered with humanity. Endow also our enemies with enlightened minds, that they may become sensible of their injustice, and willing to restore our liberty and peace. Grant the petition of thy servant for the sake of Him whom thou hast called thy beloved

Son; nevertheless, not my will, but thine be done. Amen."

The next morning, the traveler, declining the pressing solicitations to breakfast with his host, declared it was necessary for him to cross the river immediately; at the same time offering a part of his purse, as a compensation for the attention he had received, which was refused.

"Well, sir," concluded he, "since you will not permit me to recompense you for your trouble, it is but just that I should inform you on whom you have conferred so many obligations, and also add to them by requesting your assistance in crossing the river. I had been out yesterday, endeavoring to obtain some information respecting our enemy, and being alone, ventured too far from the camp; on my return I was surprised by a foraging party, and only escaped by my knowledge of the roads and the fleetness of my horse. My name is George Washington."

Surprise kept the listener silent for a moment; then, after unsuccessfully repeating the invitation to partake of some refreshment, he hastened to call two Negroes, with whose assistance he placed the horse on a small raft of timber that was lying in the river near the door and soon conveyed the General to the opposite side, where he left him to pursue his way to the camp, wishing him a safe and prosperous journey. On his return to the house he found that while he was engaged in making preparations for conveying the horse across

the river his illustrious visitor had persuaded his
wife to accept a token of remembrance, which
the family are proud of exhibiting to this day
[1835].[17]

EARLY MORNING PRAYER

Here is another instance of General
Washington's habit of prayer, witnessed
during the war:

In the year 1820, a clergyman of his state
[Virginia], being in company with Major
Lewis, a nephew of General Washington,
had an accidental conversation with him on
the subject of Christianity. The conversation
was of a controversial nature in the beginning, and as no good seemed to ensue, but
some warmth of feeling, an effort was made
to arrest the unprofitable discussion by an
inquiry made of the Major, as to the religious opinions of his distinguished kinsman.
This was done in part as knowing his vene-
ration for Washington, and for information
too, as he had been captain of the General's
bodyguard during the greater part of the
war, and possessed the best opportunities of
learning his views and habits. In answer to
the question, he observed, after hesitating for

a moment, "General Washington was certainly a pious man, his opinions being in favor of religion, and his habits all of that character and description." Being further interrogated as to his habits, he replied that his uncle, he knew, was in the habit of praying in private; and with the animation of an old soldier, excited by professional recollections rather than sympathy with the subject, he related the circumstances of the following occurrence:

While encamped at (year and place forgotten by the writer), New Jersey, a soldier arrived one morning, about daybreak, with despatches for the Commander-in-chief from a distant division of the army. As soon as his business was known he was directed to me as captain of the bodyguard, to whom he came forthwith, and giving me his papers, I repaired at once to the General's quarters. On my way to his room after reaching the house I had to go along a narrow passage of some length. As I approached his door, it being yet nearly dark, I listened for a moment, when I distinguished the General's voice, and in another moment found that he was engaged in audible prayer. As in his earnestness he had not heard my footsteps, or if he heard me did not choose to be interrupted, I retired to the front of the dwelling, till such time as I supposed him unengaged; when returning, and no longer hearing his voice, I knocked at the door, which being promptly opened, I delivered the despatches, received an answer, and dismissed the soldier.[18]

LITTLE GIRLS HEAR PRAYER

A writer says that the Rev. D. D. Field mentioned to her the following:

Mrs. Watkins, a daughter of Governor Livingston, being at my house in Stockbridge, some twenty years since [this was published in 1857], said that when she was a girl General Washington lived four months at her father's during the Revolution, and that she had been by the side of his room and heard him at prayer. My impression is that he did this repeatedly. She said that his room was in a distant part of the building, and that she had to pass through several rooms to get by the side of the General's room. She stated that her sisters used to go with her and listen, and that their father, learning what they were doing, checked them for it.[19]

SAW HIM PRAYING

General Robert Porterfield, who was brigade-inspector under General Washington in the Revolution, told General S. H. Lewis that "upon one occasion, some emergency (which he mentioned) induced him to dispense with the usual formality, and he went directly to General Washington's apartment, where he found him on his knees, engaged in morning devotions. He said that he mentioned the circumstances to General Hamilton, who replied that such was his constant habit."[20]

Heard Him Pray

Mr. Cornelius Doremus, who as a boy was fond of waiting on Washington, who lived part of a winter (1781) at his father's house in Pequannock, New Jersey, states that his bedchamber was directly over that of the Commander-in-chief, and that he often distinctly heard the sound of that deep and earnest voice in private prayer.[21]

Family Prayers

"Washington had prayers morning and evening and was regular in attendance at the church in which he was a communicant."[22]

Grace at Table

Washington was in the habit of asking the divine blessing at his table. On one occasion, from the force of habit, he performed

LIBRARY
St. Mary's Seminary - Junior College

this duty when a clergyman was present—
an instance of indecorum quite unusual with
him.   Being told of the incivility, after the
minister's departure, he expressed his regret
at the oversight, but added, "The reverend
gentleman will at least be assured that we
are not entirely graceless at Mount Vernon."[23]

When Mrs. Washington arrived in New
York after Washington's inauguration, the
President gave a semi-official dinner. From
one who was present (Mr. Wingate) we
have the following account:

The guests consisted of the Vice-President, the
foreign ministers, the heads of departments, the
speaker of the House of Representatives, and the
senators from New Hampshire and Georgia, the
then most Northern and Southern states. It was
the least showy dinner that I ever saw at the
President's table, and the company was not large.
As there was no chaplain present, the President
himself said a very short grace as he was sitting
down.[24]

When a minister of the gospel was
present, he requested him to officiate. The
Rev. Ashabel Green, who was one of the
chaplains of Congress from 1792 to 1800,

says, "It was the usage under President Washington's administration that the chaplain of Congress should dine with him once in every month when Congress was in session." He mentions, "that the place of the chaplain was directly opposite to the President. The company stood while the blessing was asked, and on a certain occasion the President's mind was probably occupied with some interesting concern, and on going to the table he began to ask a blessing himself. He uttered but a word or two, when, bowing to me," says Dr. Green, "he requested me to proceed, which I accordingly did. I mention this," he continues, "because it shows that President Washington always asked a blessing himself when a chaplain was not present."[25]

In some reminiscences of Washington, Dr. Green states that "he always, unless a clergyman was present, at his own table, asked a blessing, in a standing posture. If a clergyman were present, he was requested both to ask a blessing and to return thanks after dinner."[26]

The artist, Sharples, who spent some time at Mount Vernon painting Washington's picture, says: "I take all my meals with the Chief at Mount Vernon; they are most elegantly served, but without the least profusion, and the attendance is of military precision. I observed that we never partook of food without the General offering grace to the Giver, so also at the close of every repast."[27]

PRIVATE DEVOTIONS

Probably few Christians have been more attentive to their private devotions, at all times and in all circumstances. No matter how urgent the business which engaged his attention, he never forgot his daily dependence upon God, and that his favor must be sought in earnest prayer.

(1) *Colonel B. Temple*

Colonel B. Temple, one of his aides in the French and Indian War, said that, on sudden and unexpected visits to his marque, he "more than once found him on his knees at his devotions."[28]

(2) *Bishop Meade*

Bishop Meade, of the Episcopal Church,

who was bishop of Virginia for thirty-three
years (1829-1862), says:

It may most positively be affirmed that the impression on the minds of his family was that when
on each night he regularly took his candle and
went to his study at nine o'clock and remained
there until ten, it was for the purpose of reading
the Scriptures and prayer. It is affirmed by more
than one that he has been seen there on his knees
and also been heard at his prayers. In like manner it is believed that when at five o'clock each
morning, winter and summer, he went to that
same study, a portion of time was then spent in
the same way. It is also well known that it was
the impression in the army that Washington,
either in his tent or in his room, practiced the
same thing. One testifies to having seen him on
more than one occasion thus engaged on his
bended knees. It is firmly believed that when in
crowded lodgings at Valley Forge, where every-
thing was unfavorable to private devotions, his
frequent visits to a neighboring wood were for
this purpose.[29]

(3) *Nelly Custis*

Nelly Custis was the granddaughter of
Mrs. Washington, and the adopted daughter
of General Washington. She lived for
twenty years in Washington's family. February 26, 1833, she wrote a letter to Mr.

Jared Sparks, the historian, in which she says:

It was his custom to retire to his library at nine or ten o'clock, where he remained an hour before he went to his chamber. He always rose before the sun, and remained in his library until called for breakfast. I never *witnessed* his private devotions. I never *inquired* about them. I should have thought it the greatest heresy to doubt his firm belief in Christianity. His life, his writings prove that he was a Christian. He was not one of those who act or pray, "that they may be seen of men." He communed with his God in secret.[30]

(4) *Robert Lewis*

Mr. Sparks adds the following:

It seems proper to subjoin to this letter what was told to me by Mr. Robert Lewis, at Fredericksburg [Virginia], in the year 1827. Being a nephew of Washington and his private secretary during the first part of his Presidency, Mr. Lewis lived with him on terms of intimacy, and had the best opportunity for observing his habits. Mr. Lewis said he had accidentally witnessed his private devotions in his library both morning and evening; that on those occasions he had seen him in a kneeling posture with a Bible open before him, and that he believed such to have been his daily practice. Mr. Lewis is since dead, but he was a gentleman esteemed for his private worth and respectability. I relate the anecdote as he told it to me, understanding at the time that he was willing it should be made public on his authority. He added, that it was the President's custom to go to his library in the morning at four o'clock, and that, after his devotions, he usually spent his time till breakfast in writing letters.[31]

(5) *Military Family*

"Throughout the war, as it was understood in his military family, he gave part of every day to private prayer and devotion."[32]

DEPORTMENT IN CHURCH

His demeanor in church was always reverential and devout. He bore his part in the response, and bowed his head at the mention of the name of Jesus in the Creed.

The Rev. Lee Massey, rector of Pohick Church, where Washington was a member, expressed himself in the following strain: "His behavior in the house of God was ever so deeply reverential that it produced the happiest effects on my congregation, and greatly assisted me in my pulpit labors."[33]

The Rev. William White, D.D., rector of Christ Church, Philadelphia, which Washington attended when a member of the Continental Congress, says, "His behavior was always serious and attentive."[34]

Major Popham served under General Washington during the Revolutionary War. He attended Saint Paul's Church, New York, during the entire period of Washington's residence in New York as President of the United States. He occupied a pew next to that of the President, and sat near him. He says:

The steady seriousness of his manner, the solemn, audible, and subdued tone of voice in which he read and repeated the responses, the Christian humility which overspread and adorned the native dignity of the saviour of his country, at once exhibited him a pattern to all who had the honor of access to him.[35]

On Christmas day, 1783, Washington attended a service in the Episcopal church, at Alexandria, Virginia, "and no one bowed in deeper gratitude than the great general, who came as humbly as a little child to this, his Father's house."[36]

One who attended Christ Church, Philadelphia, when that city was the capital, gives his impressions of President Washington at church: "The deportment of Washington was reverent and attentive; his eyes, when not on the prayerbook, were on the officiating clergyman, and no witless or irreverent worshiper could plead Washington's example."[37]

A lady visiting in Alexandria, Virginia, thus describes Washington in church: "He walked to his pew, at the upper part of the church, and demeaned himself throughout the services of the day with that gravity and propriety becoming the place and his own high character."[38]

Nelly Custis, his adopted daughter, says, "No one in church attended to the service with more reverential respect."[39]

Dorothy Dudley, in her diary of January 1, 1776, makes note of the service in Christ Episcopal Church, Cambridge, Massachusetts, the day before, saying, "The General's majestic figure bent reverently in prayer as with devout earnestness he entered into the service."[40]

Stood During Prayer

Washington Irving, in his *Life of George Washington,* says, "Mrs. Washington knelt during the prayers; he always stood, as was the custom at that time."[41]

Nelly Custis says: "My grandmother, who was eminently pious, never deviated from her early habits. She always knelt. The General, as was then the custom, stood during the devotional parts of the service."[42]

Church Membership

Washington and Mrs. Washington were both communicants of the Protestant Episcopal Church. In conversation with Rev. Dr. Johnes of Morristown, New Jersey, concerning the Lord's Supper, Washington, referring to himself, said, "Though a member of the Church of England, I have no exclusive partialities." When he was passing through Litchfield, Connecticut, during the war, he saw some of his soldiers throw stones at the church, and at once rebuked them, saying with much personal feeling, "I am a churchman, and wish not to see the church dishonored and desolated in this manner."

In 1835 the Rev. E. C. M'Guire, rector of the Episcopal church at Fredericksburg, Virginia, writes as follows:

Among the aged persons residing in the neighborhood of Mount Vernon, and the descendants of such others as have recently gone down to the grave, there is but one opinion in regard to the fact of his having been a communicant in the Pohick Church, previous to the Revolutionary War. The writer himself had it from a respectable lady that she had once heard her mother unqualifiedly declare that General Washington was a communicant in that church, in the vicinity of which she had her residence, and on the services of which she attended. A living granddaughter of the Rev. Lee Massey, rector of Mount Vernon Parish for some years after Washington's marriage, says her grandfather on a special occasion told her the same thing in answer to a particular inquiry on the subject.[43]

George Washington Parke Custis, his adopted son, says, "Washington was a member in full communion of the Protestant Episcopal Church."[44]

General Robert Porterfield, Augusta, Georgia, brigade-inspector under General Washington in the Revolution, said to General S. H. Lewis, "General Washington was a pious man, and a member of your church" [Episcopal].[45]

CHURCH ATTENDANCE

Until he was eleven years old George went with his parents to the Church of England, in Truro Parish, Virginia, of which his father was a vestryman from 1735 to 1743.

The next three years he lived with his half-brother, Augustine, in Westmoreland (Virginia), and regularly attended public worship at the parish church, known then and now as Pope's Creek Church.

The next two years, 1746 to 1748, he divided his time between the home of his brother Lawrence, at Mount Vernon, and his mother, opposite Fredericksburg, Virginia, where, in company with his mother, he shared the benefits of divine worship.

From 1748 to 1759 there was little church-going for the young surveyor or soldier, but after his marriage in 1759, he and Mrs. Washington selected as their regular place of worship Pohick Church, seven miles west of Mount Vernon. October 25, 1762, he was elected one of the vestrymen of Truro Parish, which contained three churches—Pohick, Falls and Alexandria. He was first appointed church warden, October 3, 1763. He served as a member of the vestry continuously for twenty years. Church wardens were elected each year, and Washington held the office for three terms at least in ten years.

In 1773 a new church building was completed in Alexandria, ten miles north of Mount Vernon. Washington bought a pew, and attended this church frequently before the Revolution.

His adopted son, George Washington Parke Custis, says, "He always attended divine service in the morning" [when the weather and the roads permitted a ride of seven or ten miles].

The Rev. Lee Massey, rector of Pohick Church, says:

I never knew so constant an attendant on church as Washington. . . . No company ever withheld him from church. I have often been at Mount Vernon on the Sabbath morning when his breakfast table was filled with guests, but to him they furnished no pretext for neglecting his God, and losing the satisfaction of setting a good example. For, instead of staying at home, out of false complaisance to them, he used constantly to invite them to accompany him.[46]

During the Revolutionary War, interruptions sometimes occurred which prevented the holding of divine service in camp. They were not allowed to interfere, however, with the Commander-in-chief's attention to the duty, for one of his secretaries, Judge Harrison, has often been heard to say that "whenever the General could be spared from camp on the Sabbath, he never failed riding out to some neighboring church, to join those who were publicly worshiping the Great Creator."[47] As far as possible, he was regular in his habits of devotion.

"During the war he not unfrequently rode ten or twelve miles from camp to attend public worship; and he never omitted this attendance when opportunity presented."[48]

During both winters that the army was encamped at Morristown, New Jersey, Washington was a constant attendant on the preaching of the Rev. Dr. Timothy Johnes, in the Presbyterian Church.

While giving his regular attendance after the war to Christ Episcopal Church, Alexandria, Virginia, it was his custom to visit and worship at Falls Church at least four times a year, this being a part of his parish [Fairfax]. Occasionally he visited P o h i c k Church.

It is said that early on the morning of Inauguration Day, April 30, 1789, Washington went alone to Saint Paul's Church, New

York, to ask that divine wisdom and strength might be his as he assumed his new responsibilities.

After the inaugural address, he proceeded with the whole assembly on foot to Saint Paul's Church, where divine service was celebrated by Bishop Provoost, of the Protestant Episcopal Church.

While President he was most punctual in his attendance on the public worship of God, whenever it was possible. In New York he attended Saint Paul's and Trinity Episcopal Churches.

The Rev. E. C. M'Guire married the daughter of Mr. Robert Lewis, the nephew and private secretary of Washington, and thus had exceptional sources of information. He says:

In December, 1790, Congress met at Philadelphia, and the President, of course, removed there [August 30, 1790]. His conduct continued to be distinguished by the same uniform and punctual observance of religious duties which has always marked his life. He had a pew in Christ Church of that city, of which the venerable Bishop White was then the rector. During all the time that he was in the government Washington was punctual in his attendance on divine worship.

His pew was seldom vacant when the weather would permit him to attend.[49]

When in Philadelphia attending the Continental Congress, as well as during the Revolutionary War and when he was President, he attended Christ Episcopal Church.

George Washington Parke Custis, of Arlington, Virginia, adopted son of Washington and grandson of Mrs. Washington, says, "On Sundays, unless the weather was uncommonly severe, the President and Mrs. Washington attended divine service at Christ Church [Philadelphia]."[50]

Nelly Custis says, "In New York and Philadelphia he never omitted attendance at church in the morning, unless detained by indisposition."[51]

One winter, however (1781-2), being in Philadelphia in connection with some measures before Congress, he attended regularly Saint Peter's Episcopal Church, having rented a house near that church.[52]

Bishop White, rector of Christ Church, Philadelphia, when Washington resided there, says:

During his Presidency our vestry provided him with a pew not ten yards in front of the desk. It was habitually occupied by himself, by Mrs. Washington, who was a regular communicant, and by his secretaries.[53]

After his retirement from the chair of state, Washington still continued his religious habits in spirit and practice. The church in Alexandria was again his place of worship. The distance, indeed, was ten miles, and yet his pew was seldom unoccupied on the Lord's Day.[54]

CHURCHES ATTENDED

In childhood and youth, and while at home at Mount Vernon, it is known that Washington worshiped in the following churches (Church of England, later known as Protestant Episcopal):

Yeocomico Church, Westmoreland, Virginia.

Pope's Creek Church, Westmoreland, Virginia.

Saint Peter's Church, New, Kent, Virginia.

Pohick Church, Truro Parish, Virginia.

Falls Church, Truro Parish, Virginia.

Payne's Church, Fairfax County, Virginia.

Christ Episcopal Church, Alexandria, Virginia.

Saint George's Church, Fredericksburg, Virginia.

In the course of his military and Presidential travels about the country, at various times he attended service in the churches (Episcopal), most of which can be substantiated from his diary:

Trinity Church, Boston, Massachusetts.

Trinity Church, New Haven, Connecticut.

Christ Church, Cambridge, Massachusetts.

Trinity Church, New York City.

Saint Paul's Church, New York City.

Christ Church, Philadelphia, Pennsylvania.

Saint Peter's Church, Philadelphia, Pennsylvania.

Trinity Church, Newport, Rhode Island.

Queen's Chapel of Saint John's Church, Portsmouth, New Hampshire.

Bruton Church, Virginia (in the parish register his name occurs eleven times).

Saint Philip's Church, Charleston, South Carolina.

Saint Michael's C h u r c h , Charleston, South Carolina.

Christ Church, Savannah, Georgia.

He attended service in churches of other denominations also, as recorded in his diary:

September 25, 1774. Quaker Church, Philadelphia, Pennsylvania.

October 9, 1774. Presbyterian Church, Philadelphia, Pennsylvania.

July to December, 1775. Congregational Church, Cambridge, Massachusetts.

Winter, 1776-77. Presbyterian Church, Morristown, New Jersey.

May 20, 1781. Congregational Church, Wethersfield, Connecticut.

October 31, 1783. Princeton College Chapel, Princeton, New Jersey.

May 26, 1787. Roman Catholic Church, Philadelphia, Pennsylvania.

O c t o b e r 18, 1789. Congregational Church, New Haven, Connecticut.

O c t o b e r 25, 1789. Congregational Church, Boston, Massachusetts.

November 1, 1789. Presbyterian Church, Portsmouth, New Hampshire.

N o v e m b e r 8, 1789. Congregational Church, Perkins' Tavern, Connecticut.

July 3, 1791. Dutch Reformed Church, Lancaster, Pennsylvania.

October 5, 1794. Presbyterian Church, Carlisle, Pennsylvania.

COMMUNION SERVICE

Washington "partook regularly of the communion service until he entered the office of general in the American army."[55]

It was the custom in the colonial churches to administer communion only at Christmas, Easter, and Whitsuntide, and it was not an uncommon practice for communicants to receive only once a year.

Nelly Custis says:

My mother resided two years at Mount Vernon, after her marriage with John Parke Custis, the only son of Mrs. Washington. I have heard her say that General Washington always received the sacrament with my grandmother [Mrs. Washington] before the Revolution.[56]

The Rev. Thomas Chapman, in a volume of his sermons, says:

From the lips of a lady of undoubted veracity, yet living [1835] and a worthy communicant of the church, I received the interesting fact that soon after the close of the Revolutionary War *she saw him* [Washington] partake of the consecrated symbols of the body and blood of Christ, in Trinity Church, in the city of New York.[57]

Major Popham served under General Washington in the Revolutionary War. He attended Saint Paul's Church in New York when Washington resided there as President and attended the same church. He says:

The President had more than once—I believe I may say often—attended at the sacramental table, at which I had the privilege and happiness to kneel with him. And I am aided in my associations by my elder daughter, who distinctly recollects that her grandmama, Mrs. Morris [wife of the Chief Justice], often mentioned that fact with great pleasure.[58]

General Robert Porterfield, of Augusta, Georgia, who was brigadier-inspector under General Washington in the Revolution, says, "I saw him myself on his knees receive the sacrament of the Lord's Supper in [Christ] Church, in Philadelphia."[59]

LORD'S SUPPER IN APPLE ORCHARD

The following story was first published in Doctor Hosack's *Life of DeWitt Clinton* in 1829, and related in the words of the Rev. Samuel H. Coxe, D.D. (pastor of Laight Street Presbyterian Church, New York City), and father of the late Bishop Coxe, of the Episcopal Church. Doctor Coxe received the account from Doctor Hillyer, who had it directly from Dr. Timothy Johnes:

"I have the following anecdote," says Doctor Coxe, "from unquestionable authority. It has never, I think, been given to the public; but I received it from a venerable clergyman, who had it from the lips of the Rev. Dr. Jones [Johnes] himself. To all Christians, and to all Americans, it cannot fail to be acceptable."

While the American army, under the command of Washington, lay encamped at Morristown, New Jersey [winter 1776-7], it occurred that the service of the communion [then observed semiannually only] was to be administered in the Presbyterian church of that village. In a morning of the previous week the General, after his accustomed inspection of the camp, visited the house of the Rev. Dr. Jones [Johnes], then pastor of the church, and, after the usual preliminaries, thus accosted him:

"Doctor, I understand that the Lord's Supper is to be celebrated with you next Sunday. I would learn if it accords with the canon of your church to admit communicants of another denomination?"

The Doctor rejoined, "Most certainly; ours is not the Presbyterian table, General, but the Lord's table; and hence we give the Lord's invitation to all his followers, of whatever name."

The General replied, "I am glad of it; that is as it ought to be; but, as I was not quite sure of the fact, I thought I would ascertain it from yourself, as I propose to join with you on that occasion. Though a member of the Church of England, I have no exclusive partialities."

The Doctor reassured him of a cordial welcome, and the General was found seated with the communicants the next Sabbath.[60]

Why in an apple orchard? There was a vast amount of sickness in the army, a scourge of smallpox, and other fatal diseases. The Presbyterian and Baptist churches, and the courthouse, were occupied as hospitals. There was no place for the meetings of the congregation except in the open air. They were conducted in the apple orchard in the rear of the Presbyterian manse.[61]

In the orchard there is a natural basin several feet deep, and a few rods in diameter. The basin was formerly considerably deeper than at present, having been partly filled in the process of tilling ever since the Revolution. When the people assembled for worship, they occupied the bottom of that basin for their place of meeting. The minister stood on one side of the basin, so as to be elevated above his congregation. The whole field inclines toward the morning and midday sun. The rising grounds in the rear would, to a great extent, shield the congregation from the usual winds of winter. Indeed, the basin was formerly so deep that the wind from any direction would mainly pass over them.[62]

Washington at the Communion Table

It is the Sabbath. The congregation are assembled in an orchard, in a natural basin which Providence had made for them, to pay their homage to the Most High, and to commemorate even in the winter the love of the Redeemer. Among their number is the Commander-in-chief of the American army. With a willing and devout spirit he unites with the people of God in the ordinances of religion. After a solemn sermon from a venerable minister, a hymn is sung, and the invitation given to the members of sister churches to unite in the celebration of the Lord's Supper. A well-known military form rises in response to the invitation. With solemn dignity and Christian meekness he takes his seat with Christ's people and partakes of the bread and wine. It is Washington at the communion table.[63]

Sunday Devotions at Home

George Washington Parke Custis says that it was Washington's custom at Mount Vernon, after attending church in the morning, to "read a sermon or some portion of the Bible to Mrs. Washington in the afternoon."[64]   At Philadelphia, while President, he says, "And in the evenings the President read to Mrs. Washington, in her chamber, a sermon, or some portion from the Sacred Writings."[65]   Bishop Meade says, "It is also a fact well known to the family that, when prevented from public worship, he used to read the Scriptures and other books with Mrs. Washington in her chamber."[66]

"Sometimes he would sit as if he forgot that he was not alone and raising his hand would move his lips evidently in prayer."[67] "I have often seen him perfectly abstracted, his lips moving, but no sound was perceptible," says Nelly Custis.[68]

Last Private Prayer

"Feeling that the hour of his departure out of this world was at hand, he desired that everybody would quit the room.   They all

went out; and, according to his wish, left him
—with his God.

"There, by himself, like Moses alone on
the top of Pisgah, he seeks the face of God."[69]

It seems that he desired to be alone a little
while for private prayer.

DYING PRAYER

"Feeling that the silver cord of life is
loosing, and that his spirit is ready to quit
her old companion, the body, he extends himself on his bed—closes his eyes for the last
time with his own hands—folds his arms
decently on his breast, then breathing out,
'Father of mercies, take me to thyself,'—he
falls asleep."[70]

MRS. WASHINGTON PRAYS

Mrs. Washington's grandson, George
Washington Parke Custis, who lived at
Mount Vernon, says:

In that last hour, prayer was not wanting at
the throne of grace. Close to the couch of the
sufferer, resting her head upon that ancient book,
with which she had been wont to hold pious communion a portion of every day for more than
half a century, was the venerable consort [Mrs.
Washington] absorbed in silent prayer.[71]

Mrs. Washington's Prayer Life

Mrs. Washington's grandson, George Washington Parke Custis, who was adopted by Mr. Washington when he was six months old, and who was in his nineteenth year when Washington died, says of his grandmother's lifelong habit, "After breakfast she retired for an hour to her chamber, which hour was spent in prayer and reading the Holy Scriptures, a practice that she never omitted during half a century of her varied life."[72]

Nelly Custis, her granddaughter, says, "She never omitted her private devotions or her public duties."[73]

His Mother's Prayers

It was the habit of Washington's mother, during the latter years of her life, to repair daily to a secluded spot near her dwelling, formed by overhanging rocks and trees. There, isolated from worldly thoughts and objects, she sought, in devout prayer and meditation, most appropriate preparation for the great change which she was admonished by her advanced age might nearly await her. (She died August 25, 1789, at the age of eighty-two.)

Probably it was here that she wrote the prayers, religious thoughts, and experiences which she sent to her son George during the Revolutionary War.

Prior to the Revolutionary War the mercantile house of Robert Cary & Co., of London, acted as agents and correspondents of Washington, then an officer in the British service. Robert Cary was a warm friend and admirer of Washington, and did much in England to bring about a better understanding of Washington and the new nation in America. Washington entertained for him a feeling akin to affection, and made him his confidant.

Among the Cary papers has been found a copy of what is designated through a memorandum docketing them, as the "Religious thoughts and experiences of Mary Washington, given to her son George, and which, in an hour of thankfulness to the Almighty for the nation's deliverance from great peril, is transmitted to Robert Cary as a thank-offering for earnest, cordial help."

No further explanation is traceable, nor, indeed, in the mind of the writer is any needed, regarding these fervent, heartfelt expressions, sought by an earnestly religious mother to be impressed on her son.

The early loss of husband and child was a trial such as poor, frail humanity could not have borne without the special grace of God the Comforter. True it is that our greatest griefs spring from our holiest and best joys. In her family affections God bestowed on Mary Washington the highest of all earthly good things. Like her son, her highest pleasures were found in duty. Let none who read these her "thoughts and experiences" deem her other than the wonderfully cheerful spirit she in truth was. To her all life was happy, and one marked feature in her beautiful character was that she thoroughly enjoyed life, largely traceable to her having found enjoyment in every duty which she had to perform. Let none henceforth say of this grand woman that "little is known of her." It may more truthfully be said, "Of whom know we so much?"

No mention is made in the Cary papers as to any occasions of these meditations, beyond those called forth by Lord Cornwallis' surrender.

(1)

The following message was received by George Washington from his mother after the surrender of Lord Cornwallis:

Truly does this event proclaim that the Great Sovereign of heaven and earth governs the world. There are no accidents of fortune. Things are not left to the wills of men, to blind chance, to their own contingency, but are all inspired, guided, and ordered by Him. *He* is still the same, and will order all things well. No snares, intrigues, or difficulties puzzle or prevent the ways and purposes of God. Whatsoever contrivances and confusions be amongst men, He still keeps His throne, never lets loose of the reins of His government of the world, though the instruments of His overruling power may be guilty of violence and injustice. *If thou seest the oppression of the poor, and violent preventing of judgment and justice in a province, marvel not at the matter, for He that is higher than the highest, regardeth; and there be higher than they.* The tragical rents and revolutions of states and kingdoms, the disappointment of councils, the defeats of armies long flushed with success, the dissolving of majesty, the pulling asunder the thrones of mighty empires, the numerous accidents and travesties of human life, all depend upon the disposing will and pleasure of God.

They who continually make God their defense, that trust to His protection, rely and cast themselves upon Him for safety, shall find Him a sure safeguard; they are His particular care and charge, under His special providence and defense, secure from all hurt and danger; He that dwelleth in the secret places of the Most High, shall abide under the shadow of the Almighty. He shall cover thee with His feathers, and under His wings shalt thou trust. He loves us better than we love ourselves, and better knows what is fit for our interest, our universal welfare, which is lodged more intimately in His heart than it can be in ours. Although our sins deserve Thy wrath, and nothing that we can do deserves Thy favor, yet *godliness hath the promise of the life which is to come.* It was Thy errand into the world to save us from perishing. Thou art effectively the Saviour of the body. And shall we not trust Thee in what Thou hast undertaken, who trust man if we judge him faithful?

(2)

In an hour of national despondency his mother had sent him the following:

O Merciful Saviour, how have I been blessed by Thee in the enjoyment of calmness and resignation during times of trouble and perplexity, arising through the prospects and prognostics of approaching miseries; when men's hearts were failing them for fear, and for looking after those things they feared to be coming upon them. Thou gavest me inward *peace* and *rest*, which *they* can never possess, who entertain *evil tidings* with dismayed minds, and have nothing to trust to, or rest upon, but what may be damaged or taken from them. *Fear of future trouble* is the great disturber of human life, molests our quiet hours with dismal apprehensions; prevents not, nor eases, an expected calamity; torments us before it comes, more than the calamity itself.

External comforts or crosses should make little accession to, or diminution from, the satisfaction and serenity of our spirits. It is far better not to *need*, to be above, than to *enjoy abundance*. *All* is well so long as it is well *within*. When *Simeon* had the *Infant Saviour* in his arms, and *Zacchæus Christ* in his house, how little were they taken with, or concerned for, other things. It is not *abundance* men need, but *satisfied minds*. For wealth, none are nearer happiness nor further from the grave. In the twinkling of an eye all are turned out of the world, as naked as they came into it. A few fleet moments make but a little difference. God is too *just* to do us wrong, too *good* to do us hurt, and too *wise* not to know what will do us good or hurt.

(3)

Her heart is open to the sufferers from

the war, and she points them to the supreme
Sufferer for mankind:

O merciful Saviour, comfort the hearts of all
whom Thou honorest to suffer for their country's
sake in these days of peril and uncertainty. Open
our hearts to share their sorrows, and be it our
privilege to make sacrifices for their sakes. Con-
sidering our great *examples of suffering and
patience,* how can we be *impatient sufferers?* Who
can be troubled at want, that worships a God
willing to live and die in sorrow? Undervalued,
traduced, envied, reproached, betrayed, aban-
doned, put to death by His countrymen. His
tribute paid by a fish; His triumphs solemnized
by another age's colt; born among beasts, lived
among publicans, died among thieves; His birth
without a cradle; His burial without a rag or
grave of His own; and the price of His blood
buys a burial-place for strangers. Why wouldst
Thou be thus homely, but that by contemning
worldly glory, Thou mightest teach us to do so,
and sanctify *poverty* unto them, whom Thou call-
est unto *want;* since Thou, who hadst the choice
of all earthly conditions, wouldst be born poor,
and live despised? Who can murmur and repine
under the harshest usages, that considers Thou
(who knew all from the beginning) chosedst uncivil
men to crowd Thee with the horse and the ass
in a public stable; to have contempt thrown upon
Thy poverty? He that hath *many mansions* for
others in His Father's house hath no privacy in

an inn, and complains not, repines not at it.
He that would have given his churlish host an
eternal house in heaven for the asking, could
not have the least part of his here, because his
parents seem poor. Oh, ye suffering ones in this
world, none will have cause to complain of coarse
robes, hard bed, thin table, who call to mind how
it was with the Great King! Let us try to realize
that those *idols* of the world's esteem (riches and
honor) are so far from making us *truly happy*,
they cannot even be numbered among *good
things*.

(4)

Recognizing God's all-wise providence, she
willingly submits to his will:

We must not expect that all God's providence
in governing the world should center in our particular conveniency and happiness! Human
events and several persons' interests are so inter-
woven by Him that they have a mutual dependence
among themselves; and their meetings, which we
think *casual*, are *twice* necessary, as His decree,
and for many ends. We must consider ourselves
as pieces of the universe, and engines which that
great work, man, sets going for executing His
ends; which being all good, all means tending to
them must be so also. We must therefore bear
our crosses, not only with patience, but joy and
thankfulness, as accounting ourselves happy we
are instruments in His hand to do His work and

advance His glory; which must needs please Him, doing that willingly which others do out of constraint. How great an evil is discontent with our allotment! By desiring to have our will in such a particular we should perhaps cross God in a thousand things He hath to bring about; because it is possible a thousand things may depend upon that one thing we would have to be otherwise than it is. I will be henceforth willing to be crossed in some few things, that His work may go on in all, and His end attained or furthered in *many* things by the *one thing* I am crossed in.

(5)

That God's acts are for the good of all, is definitely recognized:

We forget that we are all servants to the same Master, who disposes all the concerns of men by an unerring wisdom, and is alone to determine the place we shall serve Him in. We think that Providence, which governs others, should only serve us, and distribute to us not what He, but ourselves think good. The common Father of mankind disposes things for the public advantage of this great family; and there cannot be a greater contempt of His wisdom than to dispute His choice. Men look upon themselves as single persons, without reference to the community whereof they are members. God hath placed none of us in so barren a soil, so forlorn a state, but there is something in it which may afford us comfort; if we husband *that* to the utmost, it is scarcely imaginable what improvement he that appears the most miserable may make of his condition.

(6)

Contentment and patience lessen suffering and increase happiness:

This *world* is a *state* of *probation;* we live *in it* on no other terms than to be liable to all the hazards and troubles, changes and vicissitudes that attend *mortality.* *Vanity* and *vexation* are the essence of all earthly things, incorporated into the mass of this visible creation. *In the world we shall have tribulation,* the ordinary lot of all those, the Captain of whose salvation was made perfect through sufferings. To be *offended* at *them,* is to be *offended* that we are *men* or *Christians.* If you be without chastisement, whereof all are partakers, then you are not sons. It is the character and brand of the wicked that *they are not in trouble as other men.* Every true Israelite expects his father *Jacob's legacy.* *The archers have sorely grieved him and shot at him and hated him.* And to find his days as his, not only *few* but *evil.* Heaven's highest favorites have no work of privilege, but the unspeakable advantage of making them easy and useful by considerate, submissive, contented minds. Patience lessens pain and suffering; trouble aggravates every sad ac-

cident; contentment makes it none at all. If we
will, it cannot harm us; if we give way to it, we
wound ourselves, and join with it to make us
miserable, and a single mischief a great many;
but if we quietly sit still, and in *patience possess
our souls*, we are what we were before the evil
came, only our souls have the addition of the
greatest joy and pleasure by the victory we have
obtained over it and ourselves. The *greatest* of
our *misfortunes* is our *impatience*. *Discontent* is
worse than any evil we feel; contentment is better
than any comfort we want or desire. How pleasant is it to a Christian to find himself willing
to be without that which he most desired; and to
suffer that to which he was most averse, far
sweeter than the obtaining and enjoying of that
he longed for!

(7)

Religion prevents many troubles and
affords support under all trials and tribu-
lations:

Impatience is our greatest misery. He that is
ever *content* with what he is, makes himself happy
without a fortune, and when others judge him
most unfortunate. While we *neglect* our *duty*,
we cannot but be troublesome to ourselves; while
we secure *that*, we cannot be much distressed in
any calamity. This, were there nothing else, is
abundantly sufficient to recommend and endear

religion to us; that the sincere observance of it not only prevents *many troubles,* but affords support under *all.* We can justly complain of nothing that separates us not from the love of God, who is perpetually concerned for human affairs, and particularly intends their *happiness* who place it only in *Him.* In a turbulent world, in unsettled times, amidst the straits and difficulties we are liable to pass through, nothing can be more desirable than to be above misfortunes, to be free from molestation and anxious thoughts, to meet all vicissitudes and events with constant equal tempers, to undergo all crosses with becoming, contented minds, to entertain the harshest accidents with equanimity and acquiescence of soul, wholly submitted unto, and fully satisfied with, the divine disposal.

How great an imposter is this world unto us! In the diversity of reports and opinions, in the eager pursuit of worldly greatness, in the hungry hunt after carnal pleasures, in the heats of passion, in the cries of the poor, in the oppression of the rich, in the throng of business, in the remission of idleness, in the diversion of friends, in spite of enemies, in the hopes and fears, joys and sorrows of this evil world, how few find rest and content! How great is the excellency of divine contentment! How necessary and profitable, pleasant and comfortable, beautiful and amiable! How it makes us rich and happy, in spite of the world, fits us to do and receive good!

(8)

The reality and the superiority of the spiritual is emphasized:

This world hath six parts of our time allowed her by God, yet still cries, "Give, give: how violently hath she urged us to encroach on the Sabbath by sitting too late the night before, or rising too early on the day after!" Alas, my soul! is this world six times more precious than Jesus, than Jehovah, that I should rob Him of His seventh part of my time for her sake? Blessed Redeemer, come up higher in my heart, and ye worldly concerns, get you down, and sit below His footstool. Lord, why should earthly cares trouble me on Thy day? Vain thoughts are sin's advocates and Thy adversaries. Oh, forgive their wickedness: and as fire melts away, so let them perish at the rebuke of Thy countenance. How long shall vain thoughts lodge within me? How long shall the august, the everlasting state of things be to my soul as a dark shadow, as the image of a dream? On this sacred morning why do I not live as just entering into eternity? as if beholding the glorious appearance of the great God my Saviour? Are not eternal things as certain now as they will be hereafter? Why, then, live I not always in the believing view, and under the deep impression of the heavens vanishing, the elements melting, the earth flaming, the angels everywhere dispersed, to gather the elect from the four

Bill Hay

BILL HAY signs Amos 'n' Andy on and off the air from Chicago even when they face a microphone in another city, which doesn't happen often.

* * *

The last time was a year and a half ago. Perhaps you don't know that Bill is manager of WMAQ, and that he announces many of that station's programs though connected with only two on the network. He also has his own hour at WMAQ, as Old Sandy.

our fire—what size 'blue c
to make a ton of coal last
satisfaction and result that
e.

'blue

T. C. Davi

900 W. 36th St.

winds of heaven, and of their ascending to meet
the Lord in the air, and be forever with Him!
What a trifle will the pleasures, honor, or wealth
of this world—nay, of a thousand worlds—be to
me then!

(9)

Her soul breaks forth in exultant praise
to God for spiritual blessings:

Reason informs me that men being made for
eternity, their time should be partly sequestrated
to the contemplation of eternal things; that, being
of a social nature, they ought to associate in their
principal business the worship of their God; and
that to avoid distraction, it is proper there should
be one fixed season of public devotion common to
all.   What a mercy for man is the Sabbath!
What weary pilgrims, wandering in pathless
deserts, were we but for this pledge of immor-
tality, whereon from inexhausted stores God pours
down His spiritual blessings on us, and whereon
we sit basking in the rays of His countenance,
forget things below, and with angels and saints
converse with Him, are warmed with love to Him,
live on Him, and in Him, and express our joy
in songs of grateful praise!   But how transcend-
ent their felicity who celebrate the everlasting
Sabbath above! who, being far removed from
weariness and pain, and rid of every evil thought,
enjoy God and the Lamb to the utmost strength of
their boundless wishes.

(10)

The Sabbath is a boon to mankind and the "emblem of eternal rest":

Awake, my soul, the wings of the morning have begun their rapid course; the early sun, the warbling birds sing their Creator's praise. Almighty Father, all things Thy name resound, Thou Eternal Cause, Supporter, End of All, wake up my soul, and join the choir: thy Maker's praise proclaim. But soft! a Maker's praise is not the half thou owest. Praise thy Redeemer— praise. On this blessed day thy Jesus rose— rose early for thy good. On this great day he finished the purchase of thy bliss; then early burst the bonds of death. Wake, wake my soul, praise thy righteousness, thy risen, thy exalted Lord!

(11)

With confidence she looks forward to the transition from earth to glory:

When we gave up ourselves to Thee, Thou becamest ours; and we did it on that condition, that Thou shouldest receive and save us. I expect, O my Saviour, but the performance of Thy covenant, and the discharge of Thy undertaken office. As Thou hast caused me to believe in Thee, to love Thee, to serve Thee, to perform the condition Thou hast laid upon me, though with many sinful failings, which Thou hast pardoned, so now

Thou wilt let my soul, which hath trusted in Thee, have the full experience of Thy fidelity; and take me to Thyself, according to Thy covenant, and remember the word unto Thy servant, upon which Thou hast caused me to hope. How many promises hast Thou left us, that we shall not be forsaken by Thee, but that we shall be with Thee where Thou art, that we may behold Thy glory![74]

SOURCE BOOKS

Following is a list of twenty-four books and sets of books from which quotations have been made. The first word is the key-word used in "Where Found," page 93.

Bancroft: *Life of Washington*, by Aaron Bancroft, 1807.

Barnes: *Christian Keepsake*, by Rev. Albert Barnes, D.D., 1840.

Burk: *Washington's Prayers*, by W. Herbert Burk, 1907. Doctor Burk very graciously gave permission to reprint these "Prayers" in this book.

Butler: *Washington at Valley Forge*, by J. M. Butler, 1858.

Clark: *Colonial Churches*, by W. M. Clark, 1907.

Custis: *Recollections and Private Memoirs of Washington*, by George Washington Parke Custis, Edited by Benson J. Lossing, 1860.

Much of the material in this book appeared in different publications as early as 1827.

George Washington Parke Custis was the grandson of Mrs. Washington. He was born in 1781. Six months later his father died. His father was the son of Mrs. Washington by a former marriage. Upon the death of his father he was adopted by General Washington, and lived with him at Mount Vernon as his own son. Mr. Custis died in 1857 in the seventy-seventh year of his age.

Dudley: *The Cambridge of 1776, With the Diary of Dorothy Dudley,* 1876.

Ford: *The True George Washington,* by Paul Leicester Ford, 1903.

Green: *The Life of Ashabel Green by Himself,* 1849.

Hosack: *Memoir of DeWitt Clinton,* by David Hosack, M.D., 1829.

Irving: *Life of George Washington,* by Washington Irving, 5 Vols., 1857.

Kirkland: *Memoirs of Washington,* by Mrs. C. M. Kirkland, 1857.

Lossing: *The Pictorial Field-Book of the Revolution,* by Benson J. Lossing, 2 Vols., 1860.

Meade: *Old Churches, Ministers and Families of Virginia,* by Bishop Meade, 2 Vols., 1872. The author was Bishop of Virginia for thirty-three years (1829-1862).

M'Guire: *The Religious Opinions and Character of Washington,* by Rev. E. C. M'Guire, 1836. Mr. M'Guire married the daughter of Mr. Robert Lewis, the nephew and private secretary of Washington, and thus he had exceptional sources of information.

Norton: *Life of General Washington,* by John N. Norton, 1870.

Potter: *Washington in His Library and Life,* by President Eliphalet Nott Potter, 1895.

Presbyterian: *The Presbyterian Magazine,* Edited

by C. Van Rensselaer, Philadelphia, Pa., February, 1851.

Scrapbook: Author's Library.

Sparks: *The Writings of George Washington*, by Jared Sparks, 12 Vols., 1834-37.

Vernon: *General Washington, the American Soldier and Christian*, by Merle Vernon.

Walter: *Memorials of Washington and Mary, His Mother, and Martha, His Wife*, by James Walter, 1887.

Weems: *The Life of General Washington*, by the Rev. Mason L. Weems, 1808.

　　Two editions were published before Washington's death. These were brief biographical sketches only. The third edition, in 1800, was dedicated to Mrs. Washington. The fourth edition was in 1804. The cherry tree, cabbage seed, and other stories, which made the book famous, first appeared in the fifth edition, in 1806.

Wylie: *Washington, A Christian*, by the Rev. Theodore Wm. John Wylie, 1862.

WHERE FOUND

The numbers correspond to the index numbers throughout the book.

The name refers to "Source Books," page 89.

[1] Burk, p. 12.
[2] Norton, p. 34.
[3] Sparks, Vol. II, p. 54.
[4] Weems, p. 182.
[5] Sparks, Vol. II, p. 54.
[6] Irving, Vol. I, p. 163.
[7] Ford, p. 29.
[8] Butler, pp. 48, 49.
[9] Irving, Vol. I, p. 461.
[10] Scrapbook, p. 84.
[11] Potter, p. 124.
[12] Lossing, Vol. II, p. 130.
[13] Weems, p. 104.
[14] Lossing, Vol. II, p. 130.
[15] Wylie, p. 29.
[16] Barnes, p. 265.
[17] M'Guire, pp. 162-167.
[18] M'Guire, pp. 160, 161.
[19] Kirkland, p. 478.
[20] Meade, Vol. II, p. 492.
[21] Kirkland, p. 479.
[22] Custis, p. 493.
[23] Norton, p. 117.

[24] Vernon, p. 44.

[25] Green, p. 267.

[26] Custis, p. 435.

[27] Walter, p. 233.

[28] Weems, p. 182.

[29] Meade, Vol. II, p. 246.

[30] Sparks, Vol. XII, p. 406.

[31] Sparks, Vol. XII, p. 407.

[32] Custis, p. 493.

[33] M'Guire, p. 141.

[34] Sparks, Vol. XII, p. 408.

[35] Meade, Vol. II, p. 490.

[36] Clark, p. 136.

[37] Kirkland, p. 486.

[38] M'Guire, p. 154.

[39] Sparks, Vol. XII, p. 405.

[40] Dudley, p. 49.

[41] Irving, Vol. I, p. 365.

[42] Sparks, Vol. XII, p. 405.

[43] M'Guire, p. 411.

[44] Custis, p. 173.

[45] Meade, Vol. II, p. 492.

[46] M'Guire, p. 141.

[47] M'Guire, p. 146.

[48] Bancroft (Aaron), p. 538.

[49] M'Guire, p. 153.

[50] M'Guire, p. 153.

[51] Sparks, Vol. XII, p. 405.

[52] Sparks, Vol. XII, p. 408.

[53] Sparks, Vol. XII, p. 408.

[54] M'Guire, p. 154.

[55] Presbyterian, p. 70.
[56] Sparks, Vol. XII, p. 406.
[57] M'Guire, p. 414.
[58] Meade, Vol. II, p. 490.
[59] Meade, Vol. II, p. 492.
[60] Hosack, p. 183.
[61] Presbyterian, Vol. I, p. 570.
[62] Presbyterian, Vol. I, p. 569.
[63] Presbyterian, Vol. I, p. 569.
[64] Custis, p. 173.
[65] M'Guire, p. 153.
[66] Meade, Vol. II, p. 246.
[67] Scrapbook, p. 85.
[68] Sparks, Vol. XII, p. 406.
[69] Weems, p. 169.
[70] Weems, p. 170.
[71] Custis, p. 477.
[72] Custis, p. 509.
[73] Sparks, Vol. XII, p. 407.
[74] Walter.

INDEX

(Headings First, in Capitals)

C